When God is Silent

When God is Silent

The 1997 Lyman Beecher Lectures on Preaching

Barbara Brown Taylor

COWLEY PUBLICATIONS

Cambridge ✦ *Boston*
Massachusetts

Published in the United States of America by Cowley Publications, a division of the Society of St. John the Evangelist. No portion of this book may be reproduced, stored in or introduced into a retrieval system, or transmitted, in any form or by any means—including photocopying—without the prior written permission of Cowley Publications, except in the case of brief quotations embodied in critical articles and reviews.

Library of Congress Cataloging-in-Publication Data:
Taylor, Barbara Brown.
    When God is silent / Barbara Brown Taylor.
        p.   cm.
    "The Beecher lectures in preaching."
    Includes bibliographical references.
    ISBN 1-56101-157-6 (alk. paper)
    1. Preaching. 2. Hidden God. 3. Communication—Religious aspects—Christianity. I. Title.
BV4222.T39 1998
251—dc21   98-4425
                                                              CIP

Cynthia Shattuck, editor; Vicki Black, copyeditor and designer
Cover photograph "Dawn, Alatna River" by Bob Waldrop.

This book is printed on recycled, acid-free paper and was produced in Canada.

Cowley Publications · 28 Temple Place
Boston, Massachusetts 02111
800-225-1534 · http://www.cowley.org/~cowley

For Fred Craddock,
who has said it all before

Contents

Preface

This little book contains the 1997 Lyman Beecher Lectures on Preaching, delivered at Yale Divinity School during the Fall Convocation that year. The original title of the work was "Famine in the Land: Homiletical Restraint and the Silence of God." The original audience included seminarians, clergy, professors, and lay people.

What we had in common was our concern for the health of Christ's body, and in particular for the role of proclamation in that body. Certainly, a preacher is not the only one who speaks in or for the church. There are other voices just as important to the vitality of the body, but insofar as a preacher's voice is heard in the context of worship, his or her speech is sanctioned in a way that other speech is not.

This is both blessing and curse, for those who listen and those who speak. It is blessing when a preacher's language rises to the occasion so that fresh revelation occurs. It is curse when the language fails to do its job and God's word is not heard. Whether a sermon is experienced as one or the other has much to do with the preacher's own abilities, but it is more than that.

Religious language is communal property, after all. None of us invents words as we speak, at least not if we wish to be understood. Instead, we dip into the great pot of our shared language about God, which includes biblical narratives, creeds, liturgies, theologies, popular piety, and folklore.

It is a pot into which quite a bit has been thrown over the years, which would lead one to expect a rich stew. Instead, many who taste it complain that it has gotten thin. Some say it is because the meat has gotten lost in all the potatoes, while others admit that they are just plain tired of stew.

The problem, for a preacher, is how to call people to the table with the language at hand, especially when so many of them have become suspicious if not downright disdainful of the spoken word. It is a problem that is compounded by God's own silence. If God spoke directly to people, then preachers could retire. As it is, God's reticence is the problem that clergy are hired to address.

That is the problem this book engages, with thanks to the many people who have engaged it with me. Most of their names are included at the back of this book, where you may find the list of sources consulted. Although I have never met most of these authors, they spoke to me as helpfully as a room full of friends.

I am especially thankful to Dean Richard Wood and the faculty of Yale Divinity School for giving me the opportunity to do this work; to Dan Moseley and Audrey Ohmen, who allowed me to tell their stories; to Paul Duke, Susannah Mosley and David Fore, who gave direction to my thinking; to Martha Sterne and Ed Taylor, who read every word of several drafts; to Peter Hawkins, who improved the manuscript; to Cynthia Shattuck and Vicki Black, who readied it for publication; to Denise Bobo, who typed it for love instead of money; and to Judy Barber, director of the Hambidge Center in Rabun Gap, Georgia, who offered me the time apart that allowed me to finish the job.

Finally, I want to thank Fred Craddock, whom I heard deliver the Beecher Lectures in 1978, and whose guiding presence has meant the world to me.

Barbara Brown Taylor
Clarkesville, Georgia

ONE

Famine

How shall I break the silence? What word is more eloquent than the silence itself? In the moments before a word is spoken, anything is possible. The empty air is formless void waiting to be addressed. Depending on what is said, earth could be all ocean, a blue waterworld in space. Adam could be a self-regenerating monk who sleeps alone by the glow of two moons, or three, and has to make his own decision about the fruit of that one beguiling tree.

Anything is possible until God exhales, inspiring the void first with wind and then with the Word, which is both utterance and act, which makes something out of nothing by saying that it is so. God says, and the *logos* yields the *cosmos*. God says, and a solemn procession of creatures steps out of the darkness, so steady on their feet that it is hard to believe they are using them for the first time. God says, and there are bats, bluebirds, fireflies, and luna moths. God says, and there are sea horses, manta rays, plankton, and clams.

But the most dangerous word God ever says is *Adam*. All by itself it is no more than a pile of dust—nothing to be concerned about, really—but by following it with the words for *image* and *dominion*, God sifts divinity into that dust, endowing it with things that belong to God alone. When God is through with it, this dust will bear the divine likeness. When God is through with it, this dust will exercise God's own dominion—not by flexing its muscles but by using its tongue.

Up to this point in the story, God has owned the monopoly on speech. Only God has had the power to make something out of nothing by saying it is so. Now, in this act of shocking generosity, God's stock goes public. "So God created humankind in his image, in the image of God he created .them; male and female he created them"—human beings endowed by God with the power of the Word.

Anyone who stands up in front of other human beings to speak knows what a frightful gift it is. This power of ours has no safety catch on it. We are as likely to make nothing out of something as the other way around. According to one survey of people's greatest fears, fear of public speaking rates much higher than fear of sickness or death.[1] The fear of self-exposure is basic to our nature, along with the fear of judgment by our peers. However well you have prepared, there is nothing like that moment of silence before you begin, when you look out at all those waiting faces and wonder if you are about to waste their time. Have you done your homework? Are your words the very best you could find? Will your body cooperate? Will your voice, your face, your spine, your hands help you make your point or contradict it? How will you break the silence? What can you say that will be more eloquent than the silence itself?

When the speech delivered happens to be a sermon, the stakes go up even higher. The conversation is no longer two-way but three-way, and the fear of judgment by one's peers takes a back seat to a more potent fear. There is a text, and a presence within the text, that wishes to be heard. The preacher must listen as well as speak, performing an act that is more complicated than solitary creation. The preacher's task is to create speech with One who has already spoken—to interpret what has already been said—so that it sings in the ear as something heard for the first time.

There are a dozen things that must go right in order for communication to occur, and not all of them are under a speaker's control. Because language is a communal act, as much depends on those who listen as on those who speak. Every word is a smoke signal sent up with great effort. The fire must be very hot. The wood must be very green. The wet blanket must be lowered and lifted at just the right moments. But none of those is any guarantee. If no one is watching the sky, you might as well be roasting marshmallows. In order for communication to occur, you need someone watching who also knows the language.

Even a knowledgeable partner is no guarantee that the message sent will be the message received. Language is porous, not solid. Every word carries its own history inside of it. A word such as *charity* does not mean the same thing now as it did a hundred years ago. Depending on a listener's own history with the word, the hearing of it may evoke a glow of contentment or a flush of shame. Send up a smoke signal that says "Practice Charity" and one person who sees it will go kiss her rebellious teenager while someone else will start rummaging through his closet for old clothes to give away. A third, who is perhaps most typical of our age, will have no context for responding to the word at all.

The inherent instability of language seems to be of more concern in literary circles than in homiletical ones. While the scholars of deconstructionism insist that even our best, most carefully chosen words are not sturdy enough to bear the truth, most preachers wield words such as *God* or *faith* as if they were made out of steel instead of air. It is not hard to understand why. Like the rest of us, those speakers rely on such language to pin down the flapping edges of the universe, even when it does not match up with all that we know to be true.

In the same way, we speak of "sunrise" and "sunset," although we know full well it is not the sun that moves. So why do we hang on to the old language? Because it describes how things actually look to us, or because the thought of "earthrise" and "earthset" gives us vertigo? The facts notwithstanding, it is easier to go to sleep at night believing that our perspective on the universe is the stable one. How could we sleep or speak either one if we could actually feel the velocity of our relentless slide through space?

What is at stake here is the sayability of the world. For millennia before now, human beings have written and spoken, read and heard words under the assumption that there was a reliable correlation between those words and the world they described. That assumption carried within it not only a belief in the reality of words—that is, in their ability to convey meaning—but also, I think, in their potential nobility. To say something well, or to hear something said well, was to reach a higher level of being (however temporarily). Why else do we have our young read Dante and Shakespeare,

Emily Dickinson and Toni Morrison, if not to expose them to words we believe will improve their lives?

And yet you know what has happened. In our lifetimes, language has taken a terrible hit. I cannot say that it has never happened before, but I do know that it is happening now—so many frontal assaults on language, on the reliability of the word that it is difficult to list them all. We may leave the complexities of deconstructionism and post-structuralism to the experts. Most of us can collect enough evidence of language in distress right where we live.

There is first of all the assault of consumerism, which forces words to make promises they cannot keep. Pressed into service on billboards, in newspaper ads, on television, and on the telephone, words are chosen not for their truthfulness but for their seductiveness. What they mean is beside the point. What they *seem* to mean is all that counts. Where I live, subdivisions spring up in cow pastures like mushrooms overnight. Since they all look the same, developers work hard to give them distinctive names. One is called "Harbor View," although the nearest body of water is thirty miles away. Another is called "Autumn Breeze," although that is only true for three months out of the year. What the words mean is beside the point. It is what they seem to mean that counts. Their value lies in the fantasies they inspire, and in the power of those fantasies to separate people from their money.

Even those of us who resist the strategy cannot save the words employed in it. Once you have bitten into a mealy, pale pink tomato, it is hard to forgive the sign that said "vine ripe." Those two words will be suspect from now on, although your tongue knows exactly what they mean. The problem is the discrepancy between the word and the reality. Because the connection has been lost, the language is no longer trustworthy. You must devise other methods for determining the truth.

While it is really a variety of consumerism, journalism has launched its own assault on language. In the case of news shows, news magazines, newspapers, and newsletters, the attack is not so much on the truthfulness of words as it is on their longevity. At my house, pounds of *The New York Times* and *Wall Street Journal* are tossed aside with whole sections unread. My guilt over this is softened by the knowledge that the newsprint will have a second life. Once a month I haul it to the county recycling center, where it is shredded into cheap bedding for local chicken houses. After the chickens are through with it, I am told, it is fed to cows who somehow benefit from the nutrients in it.

Thus yesterday's forty-eight-point headline becomes tomorrow's cow food in a process that is as pragmatic as it is strange. The moral is that there is no sense getting attached to the news, nor to the realities a reporter's words represent. How did that community recover from the hurricane? What happened to the children after their mother died of AIDS? Did the sheriff really do it or did they arrest the wrong man? Don't ask. Just let it go. There will be more stories tomorrow that are just as compelling. The word is transitory, cheap.

A third assault on the nobility of language is the sheer proliferation of words with which most of us are faced each day. Not counting taxonomic lists of species, it is estimated that the English language contains some six hundred thousand words. By comparison, Elizabethan English had about one hundred fifty thousand, and the King James Version of the Bible contains only six thousand.[2] We have words for things that were unknown a century ago—*bytes, quarks, bazookas*—and we have words that have emerged from specialized disciplines—*psychotherapy, biotechnology, econometrics.*

Predictably, perhaps, our care for words has declined as their number has increased. Children who shop at Toys R Us, and teenagers for whom the height of cool speech is that of their favorite rap artist, do not understand what the fuss is all about when their teachers point out that "quick" is not spelled q-u-i-k. The democratization of language (there is a new word for you) has had the effect of making good grammar sound fussy and the use of any word over three syllables a sure sign of the elite.

And yet the words keep coming at us through an ever-expanding variety of media—so many words that some days it sounds as if we live our lives against a wall of constant noise. For some people it is company. I know one man who keeps a television set going in every room of his house because it helps him feel less lonely. For other people noise is a weapon. Remember how the FBI broadcast Nancy Sinatra's "These Boots are Made for Walkin'" into the Branch Davidian compound in Waco in hopes of driving cult members out?

For other people, noise is frankly an addiction. The author of a recent essay in *The New York Times Magazine*, Tom Reiss, confessed that he once spent every waking hour with a Walkman headset plugged in his ears, listening to music or, more often, to educational tapes. He had a brown suede pouch for the machine that he wore around his waist. "Every morning I'd strap it on like a gunfighter's belt," he said, "low on my hip, ready to face off against my enemies: the potentially empty minutes of the day." Finally convinced that his dependence was beginning to affect his relationships, he unplugged. While he still jumps at sudden noises and often finds himself at a loss for words, he is committed to doing without his Walkman one day at a time.

The most unfortunate side-effect of all the noise is that many of us have become hard of hearing. We learn to filter out words that are not necessary to our lives the same way we learn to sleep in a house near railroad tracks. Our brains protect us from the daily barrage of words by increasing our resistance to them. Recent studies show that most people recall only about twenty-five percent of what they have heard in the past few days. We do not listen well, and at least part of it is because we can listen much faster than most people can talk.

While most human beings speak at a rate of one hundred twenty to one hundred fifty words a minute, we can process more than five hundred words a minute, which makes it hard for us to stay tuned to prolonged communication, especially if the speaker is halting or dull. We tend to use the lag time in a conversation to compose our own responses, which makes us even poorer listeners.

Kathy Thompson, who teaches courses on conversation at Alverno College in Milwaukee, was quoted in a recent article by Cynthia Crossen in *The Wall Street Journal* as saying that we have become a nation of interrupters. "At our house," Thompson says, "we warn new friends to be careful because we treat conversation like a competitive sport. The first one to take a breath is considered the listener." Psychotherapists, call-in radio hosts, and clergy all reap the benefits of this whirlwind. We are paid to listen, and people who cannot make themselves heard anywhere else in the world line up to talk to us. They may also go online, hunting chat rooms where they can log-on or log-off at will.

The personal computer has become a great boon to people who have difficulty with face-to-face communication. One man I know never leaves his house because he is embarrassed by the oxygen tank his emphysema requires him to use. He is not lonely, however. If you go to see him, you can follow his clear plastic tubing right into his bedroom, where he sits happily pecking at the keyboard of his desktop.

The computer has become a sorcerer's apprentice for the vast amount of information that is available to us each day. From my study in Clarkesville, I can view paintings that hang in the Prado in Madrid or shop for an Australian stock saddle for my quarter horse mare. The illusion of omniscience is strong. With this machine, I have access to all knowledge. The unanswerable question is a thing of the past.

One of John Updike's recent novels, *In the Beauty of the Lilies*, begins with the Reverend Clarence Wilmot, a Presbyterian minister in Paterson, New Jersey, who lost his faith one day in the spring of 1910. "The sensation was distinct," he recalled later, "a visceral surrender, a set of dark sparkling bubbles escaping upward."

Once it was gone, he sold encyclopedias for a living, but as it turned out he did not have much faith in them either. "There are twenty-five thousand separate alphabetical entries," he told one promising customer, "nearly ten thousand steel engravings. Everything you or your children want to look up, it's in there, if not as a separate article, listed in the index." When his client looked as if she might actually buy the thing, his spiel collapsed.

"You don't want it," he said. "I swear to you—it's the last thing you want. All the information there can be, and it breaks your heart at the end, because it leaves you as alone and bewildered as you were not knowing anything."[3]

What has happened to the nobility of the word? And what is left for us to believe about the sayability of the world? What words, what speakers, do we trust to tell us the truth about our lives, and how can we listen to them with such calluses on our ears?

The literary critic George Steiner, whom I thank for raising the level of my thinking about language, says we are living in the aftermath of the broken covenant between the word and the world. Until the 1870s, he says, western civilization honored a contract between *logos* and *cosmos*, the essence of which was basic human trust in the sayability of the world. While there were always breaches of that trust, we spoke and listened to each other with confidence in the ability of the word to describe the world in a truthful and meaningful way. In Steiner's estimation, that trust was broken in European, Central European, and Russian culture during the decades from the 1870s to the 1930s, resulting in a revolution of spirit which, as far as he is concerned, defines modernity itself.[4]

If that is too abstract for you, then consider Steiner's case in point: in Germany in the 1940s, we discovered that a person who can read Goethe or Rilke in the evening, who can listen to Bach and Schubert while getting ready for bed, can also get up the next morning and go to his day's work at Auschwitz. With this discovery, Steiner says, the ascendancy of the Word came to an end. "The house of classic humanism, the dream of reason which animated Western Society," largely broke down. We now live "after the Word," in a time of *epilogue*, which is both a time of endings and new beginnings.[5]

Steiner writes as a literary critic and linguist, but any preacher who reads his eulogy for the Word without sensing a chill is not paying attention. We should all be wearing black, because the assaulted, gutted word whose diminishment he laments is the same word we rely on to talk to people about God. We may capitalize "the Word" for different reasons, but it is a common language we share, and our congregations listen to us with the same ears as they listen to politicians, salespeople, and news commentators.

Their ears have been assaulted. They are fired upon every day by words intended to influence them, to manipulate them, to separate them from their cash. They are beset by more words than they can process, much less respond to, and not all of those words come from hucksters. They also come from children, spouses, co-workers, neighbors. They come from friends supporting causes and committee chairs seeking members. They come from the youth minister at the church, who needs someone to teach the sixth-grade Sunday school class this year.

Even a hermit is not safe. Every day's mail brings a handful of appeals from worthy charities. Whoever wrote them worked hard to choose words that would win a reading. Some underline paragraphs in red, while others send photographs of hungry children, abused animals, polluted rivers. There is no doubt these groups do good work. There are simply too many of them, which is why most of us have grown deaf to their pleas. With a twinge of regret, we drop them in the trash. Eventually they will make their way to the landfill where, in most places, forty percent of the garbage is paper printed with cast-off words.

Those of us who speak in churches may pretend that we are granted a privileged hearing, but in most cases we are deluding ourselves. At best, we contribute more persuasive words to a world already glutted with them. At worst, we engage in more false advertising. Every time I pass a church with a sign out front that says "Our doors and hearts are open to everyone," I think, "vine-ripe tomatoes." No church I know is open to everyone. Whom do we think we are fooling? I would so much rather see a sign that says, "We do the best we can," or better yet, "Christians meet here. Enter at your own risk."

My sister Kate, who—like me—did not grow up in the church, began attending one after her son Will was born. Trying to downplay my delight but eager to talk to her about it, I asked her one day which service they attended. "Neither one," she said. "We just go to Sunday school and then we go home." When I asked her why, she told me: how they *had* gone to church at first, and how she had sat there Sunday after Sunday listening to the preacher vent his spleen at God's enemy of the week—alcohol, the lottery, gay people, Santa Claus—until she felt as if she had been beaten with a stick.

"One day," she said, "I stood up in the middle of the sermon, put my hands over Will's ears, and led him out of the church. Now we just go to Sunday school and we're all a lot happier."

I listened to an Easter sermon once in which the preacher stood up in front of a church full of people hungry for good news and told us Easter bunny jokes, one after another. He never met our eyes. He looked up at the light fixtures as he delivered his punch lines, never noticing how we laughed less each time. Finally he said something about how Easter was God's joke on death and we should all laugh more. Then he said *Amen* and sat down. I have never in my life wished so badly for pulpit police. I wanted someone with a badge to go up and arrest that guy, slap some handcuffs on him, and lead him away.

But there is no one to stop us, you see. Some of our congregations may tactfully suggest that we take a little time off, maybe take in a preaching conference or two, but on the whole we are alarmingly free to do anything we want in the pulpit. Like most of you, I have heard the pulpit used for reviews of academic literature, true confessions, political advertisements, and one-sided arguments with members of the congregation.

I will never forget one sermon, if that is the right word, in which the preacher got up and told everyone what he did on his summer vacation. Since he was a single man who traveled alone, he was the only character in his narrative. He told us about the mountains he saw, the sheep, the sailboats, the blueberries. I kept waiting for him to connect it all to God or the gospel or even to his own soul's health, but he never did. He was just lonely, and we were the only people he could think of who might care where he went or what he did.

It reminds me of something a teacher of mine told me once. He said, "Why, I've heard preachers who get up there in the pulpit and cook up this whole big breakfast—bacon, eggs, hash browns and grits with red-eye gravy—then dang if they don't go and eat it all themselves."

I am not without sympathy for those of us who preach. We are people too, after all. We get hungry too, and some of us are starving. The problem is that nourishing words are so hard to find—words with no razor blades in them, words with no chemical additives. Most of the words offered to us have been chewed so many times there are no nutrients left in them, or else they have been left uncovered on some shelf until they are too hard to bite into. Meanwhile people look at us with their hungry eyes. As often as we have disappointed them, they never stop hoping we will give them something delicious to eat. They do not know how many of us are down to our last handful of meal, our last tablespoon of oil. They do not know that we cannot give them more than we get.

What we crave in this wilderness are fresh words from the mouth of God—not yesterday's manna, nor tomorrow's, but just enough for today. Whatever happened to the talkative God of the Bible? What wouldn't we give for one comforting word in the garden in the cool of the evening, or a commandment so audible it made people cover their heads?

Earlier this year I met a preacher who came late in her life to ordained ministry. As one of several clergy on the staff of a large urban church, she was responsible for ministry to the elderly, which included serving as chaplain to a nearby nursing home. Preaching was difficult for her, she said, because so many of her congregation lived lives of painful limitation that good news was often hard to find. She did not want to ignore their reality by focusing on the life to come, she explained, and she would not, under any circumstances, lie to them about things being any easier than they were. As a result, she found that she had little to say when it came time to preach and she was less than satisfied even with that.

At the workshop we both attended, the sermon she preached for her small group was rambling and strained. No one had to tell her so. She already knew it, and in the evaluation period that followed she spilled the truth with her tears. "I have this recurrent nightmare," she said. "I had it again last night. In the dream, I die and find myself standing before the house of God. When I knock, the door blows open and it is clear no one has lived there for a very long time. The place is vacant. There are dust balls everywhere." She looked at us, swamped with grief. "All I want is to hear God call me by name. I would give anything just to hear God say my name."

Her peers were sympathetic. At least one suggested that she find a good therapist with whom she could exorcize the spirit of that dream, and perhaps that person was right. Maybe those of us who are haunted by God's silence are blocked in some way, stopped up so that we cannot hear what we are supposed to hear. Maybe we do need professional help, but it seems entirely possible to me that what we are sensing is true. For reasons beyond our understanding, the sovereign God is not so talkative anymore.

The prophet Amos put it like this:

> The time is surely coming,
>   says the Lord GOD,
>   when I will send a famine on the land;
> not a famine of bread,
>   or a thirst for water,
>   but of hearing the words of the LORD.
> They shall wander from sea to sea,
>   and from north to east;
> they shall run to and fro,

seeking the word of the LORD,
but they shall not find it.
(Amos 8:11-12)

May I improvise? *Their prophets shall die and not be replaced. Their leaders shall speak words of promise but no power and their merchants shall fill the air with babble. Their temples shall be full of the sound of their own voices. When they pray they shall hear nothing but wind. I shall make an orphan of their mother tongue, says the Lord God. I shall let them choke on the dead husks of their own words until they beg me for fresh bread from heaven.*

I know it sounds odd to speak of famine in the land of plenty, especially when there is so much apparent evidence that God's harvest is as rich as ever. Megachurches are attracting thousands of people whom mainline churches have ignored. Movements such as Promise Keepers have given thousands more a way to practice their faith. The Christian Coalition has mobilized conservative believers to become involved in government, jolting liberals awake enough do the same thing. Whatever your valuation of these projects, they represent quite a lot of activity in the name of God. The question is, do they please God? Are numbers alone sufficient proof that the answer is "yes"? Or is discernment more difficult than counting heads?

I am not qualified to say. All I know is that where I live, a nicely landscaped neighborhood of second homes is going up one mile from the Hispanic trailer park where there are no screens on the windows. A government grant for more public housing has been turned down for fear of whom it might attract to town. When members of the Ku Klux Klan stand on the street corner in town, they hold signs that proclaim Christ as their King. A recent letter to the editor in the county newspaper praised a group of high school boys for roughing up classmates who look or act homosexual. The churches have no consensus on these things. When the county ministerial association gets together once a month, we hardly know how to speak to one another. We read the same Bible but we interpret it differently, and even within our own congregations there is hot disagreement about what God is calling us to do.

We count heads because we do not know what else to do, while our more thoughtful members leave us in search of more nourishing food.

Perhaps there is no proof a famine exists except for the fact that people are hungry. In the land of plenty, the source of that hunger can be difficult to diagnose. It is often not until we have tried to ease it with everything else we know that we discover by process of elimination our hunger for God. Our problem is not too few rations, but too many. The proof that we are in the midst of a famine of the Word are the suffocating piles of our own dead words that rise up around us on every side. It is because they do not nourish us that we require so many of them. It takes thousands of words, coming at us every moment, to distract us from the terrible silence within.

At this point in time, it is not necessary to distinguish between sacred and secular speech. Language itself is in crisis—the whole enterprise of trusting words to mean what they say, to serve as a medium of relationship and not of pretense or aggression. For those of us who confess a God we call Word made flesh, this crisis is especially grave. How can we speak of this Word with a broken language? How do we use dead words to proclaim the Word of life?

In ancient Judaism, no text containing the name of God was ever thrown away. Instead, it was laid in an underground depository called a *genizah*. The most famous of these was discovered when the great synagogue in Cairo was excavated. Inside, archaeologists found a warehouse of worn-out words—old prayer books, marriage contracts, charms and amulets, strips of Hebrew letters snipped from prayer shawls—a sepulcher of sacred words, pressed down and welded together by the weight of earth and the passage of time.[6] It was respect for those words that led people to bury them, and not to leave them lying around like so much trash.

When I see polyester T-shirts printed with full-color graphics of Jesus on the cross or receive disposable ballpoint pens printed with scripture in the mail, I wonder if it isn't time to dig a hole of our own. We have gone too far. We have presumed too much. In our garrulous efforts to proclaim the Word made flesh, we have arranged a second crucifixion. First we nailed the flesh. Now we have nailed the Word, by speaking of it too glibly. In the words of the prophet Jeremiah, we have forgotten how to blush (Jeremiah 6:15, 8:12).

At my house in the country, we start using the attic fan around June, opening the windows wide and generating our own night breeze. The only drawback is the noise. The fan is so loud I cannot hear the frogs, with an occasional whack-whack-whack that makes me dream of airplane propellers. My compromise is to put the fan on a timer so that I can wake up to the sound of birds. The first couple of nights my eyes fly open at two or three in the morning. It takes me a moment to understand why: the fan has gone off and the silence is so loud it woke me up.

In a world of too many words, silence affects people who are no longer affected by sound. Plenty of us who are defended against sound have no defense against silence. Some of us love it and some of us flee it. That is because silence can mean anything. If you come into a room where I am sitting and we do not speak, it could mean we do not know each other. It could also mean we know each other so well that words are not necessary. It could mean one of us is angry at the other, or that one of us is leaving and we are both too sad to speak. It could mean we both know the room is bugged. It could mean I am asleep.

The polyvalence of silence is what makes it so intriguing. Context is everything. The silence of a monastery is to be expected. It is one of the reasons people go there, to bathe in that quiet pool of no sound. The silence of an empty house after a divorce is something else again. Remembered voices can become ghosts that make the hair rise on the back of the neck. Turn on the television, someone. Bang pots and pans so that the silence cannot speak.

Illness is often quite silent. In between the visitors with thermometers and bouquets, there are long stretches of silence to face without the usual distractions. One may dull them with medicine or stay awake to feel things one has never felt before. The weight of flesh. The beat of blood.

The way air comes into the body cool and goes out warm, heated in the chest in the space of each breath.

In his poetic eulogy *The World of Silence*, the French philosopher Max Picard says that silence is the central place of faith, where we give the Word back to the God from whom we first received it. Surrendering the Word, we surrender the medium of our creation. We unsay ourselves, voluntarily returning to the source of our being, where we must trust God to say us once again.[7] In silence, we travel back in time to the day *before* the first day of creation, when all being was still part of God's body. It had not yet been said, and silence was the womb in which it slept.

This silence is ecumenical. It precedes dogma. It is incapable of crusades. In silence, people who do not speak the same language may yet act together, creating a tableau that talks louder than words.

In the winter of 1996, a group of Christians, Jews, Buddhists, and Sufi Muslims met in Poland for an interfaith retreat on the grounds of two old

concentration camps. Every morning they walked
an hour from Auschwitz, where they slept, to
Birkenau, where they gathered on the railroad
tracks at the center of the camp. Fifty years ago,
that was where trains from all over Europe
stopped to unload and sort their cargo. That was
where the sick were separated from the healthy,
the homosexual from the heterosexual, the
children from their parents. And that was where,
that November, one hundred fifty people from ten
countries and four world religions sat down in the
snow to remember the dead. Forming a large
ellipse about seventy-five yards long, they sat in
silent meditation twice a day, their breath curling
up around their heads in the cold air. Their
purpose was to bear witness to what happened in
that place half a century ago, but it was also to
listen for the ways in which those events still echo
in our lives today.

Some participants were surprised by joy. "I do
not yet understand," one of them said, "so I cannot
yet fully express the reasons, but we felt a complete
sense of freedom and love on those walks inside

the barbed wire. It was as if the souls of those who died were handing over to us the feelings that were prematurely taken away from them, that they never got to use themselves. This gift of life was completely unexpected."[8] On the last night of the retreat, everyone gathered in the crematorium, planting candles in the snow while some Swiss nuns led them in singing a lullaby.

There are, of course, silences of desolation as well as silences of bliss. Historically, there are the silences of Masada and Jonestown, the silences of Hiroshima and Tibet. Politically, there are the silences of those who are not allowed to speak, or who refuse to speak, because their words are so incompatible with the words of those in charge. Thomas Mann, who won the Nobel Prize for Literature in 1928, left Germany in 1938 because he knew what was happening to the German language. By carrying it into exile with him, he hoped to save it from final ruin. His countryman, Hermann Broch, did the same thing. The author of *The Death of Virgil* died in New Haven,

Connecticut, largely unknown, because he could no longer speak his own language in his own land.[9]

In the physical world of living, breathing things, complete silence means something is wrong. Even in the desert there is the occasional hum of an insect or the scrabbling of a lizard in the sand. Rachel Carson's classic work, *Silent Spring*, presents the chilling vision of a world that is quiet because all the humming, scrabbling things in it have succumbed to the poisons we humans spread around. In Africa, the Kalahari Bushmen knew their end was near when they could no longer hear the voices of the cosmos. They depended on the ringing sound of the sun, the hunting cries of the stars to confirm their place in the universe. When they could no longer hear them, it was a sign to them that their way of life on earth was over.[10]

Between human beings there may be no silence as loud as the silence of death. To sit beside a bed, day after day, listening to the ragged intake of breath—to hear the lungs fill, to hear the unproductive cough until finally there is so little need for air that there is only the slightest flutter four or five times a minute—no clock measures time like this, nor is it possible to describe the moment when there is a tick but no tock. The breath goes out and it does not come in again. No one knows it was the last until it is gone, and the silence that follows it is like no other sound in the world.

I met a man last summer—a preacher—who nursed his wife until her death, at fifty-something, from cancer. When she stopped breathing, he said, the silence in the room destroyed all language for him. No words could get into him and none could get out. He resigned from his church. Months and months later, his voice is still raspy. "It makes you want to go to Dachau," he said. "You want to go to the place where there are no answers." He did not sound angry when he said that. He sounded like someone who had been scorched by the living God and who knew better than to try and talk about it.

Christian tradition knows others who, like him, have abandoned speech: the desert fathers and mothers, the Celtic monks of the Skelligs, the

Trappists, Saint John of the Cross. We call it the *via negativa*, the negative way—not because it lacks positive virtues, but because it presumes nothing. Those who follow God down the negative way do not try to name or describe the living God. The true God is the God they cannot say. Any god they could say would be their own invention.

While this "disontology"[11] is strenuous for people who believe in divine revelation, and especially in the revelation of the Word made flesh, it is borne out in the parts of our tradition that prohibit the saying of God's name or the seeing of God's face. Scripture teaches us that both of those are life-threatening activities that only a privileged few may attempt at divinely sanctioned moments, and even then in full knowledge that they risk their lives to do so.

In this way, silence becomes God's final defense against our idolatry. By limiting our speech, God gets some relief from our descriptive assaults. By hiding inside a veil of glory, God eludes our projections. God deflects our attempts at control by withdrawing into silence, knowing that nothing gets to us like the failure of our speech. When we run out of words, then and perhaps only then can God be God. When we have eaten our own words until we are sick of them, when nothing we can tell ourselves makes a dent in our hunger, when we are prepared to surrender the very Word that brought us into being in hopes of hearing it spoken again—then, at last, we are ready to worship God.

This is my reading of our situation at the end of the twentieth century. Our language is broken. There is famine in the land. God's true name can never be spoken. What is a preacher to do? "In dispersion, the text is homeland," says George Steiner.[12] In the next chapter I want to talk about silence in the Bible, to see what can be learned.

Endnotes

1. Bert Decker, *You've Got To Be Believed To Be Heard* (New York: St. Martin's Press, 1991), 155.

2. George Steiner, *Language & Silence: Essays on Language, Literature and the Inhuman* (New York: Atheneum, 1986), 25.

3. John Updike, *In the Beauty of the Lilies* (New York: Alfred A. Knopf, 1996), 101.

4. George Steiner, *Real Presences* (Chicago: The University of Chicago Press, 1989), 93.

5. Steiner, *Language & Silence*, ix; Steiner, *Real Presences*, 94.

6. David Wolpe, *In Speech and In Silence: The Jewish Quest for God* (New York: Henry Holt and Company, 1992), 148.

7. Max Picard, *The World of Silence* (Chicago: Henry Regnery Company, 1952), 34.

8. Peter Cunningham, "Bearing Witness: Notes from Auschwitz," *tricycle* (Spring 1997), 38.

9. Steiner, *Language & Silence*, 102-103.

10. Laurens van der Post, *The Heart of the Hunter: Customs and Myths of the African Bushman* (New York: Harcourt Brace Jovanovich, 1961), 226.

11. Michael A. Sells, *Mystical Languages of Unsaying* (Chicago: The University of Chicago Press, 1994).

12. Steiner, *Real Presences*, 40.

❧ Two ❧

Silence

There are fewer and fewer oases of silence in our noisy world. Communication has higher value for us than contemplation. Information is in greater demand than reflection. There was a time when only doctors wore pagers and the only person who carried a telephone around with him was the president of the United States, in case of nuclear attack. Now we are all that important. We can be found anywhere, at anytime, by anyone who needs us. When a pager goes off in a room full of people, a banner unfurls above the wearer's head: I am necessary. I am involved in something so urgent it cannot wait.

Sometimes it is our own need to communicate that is urgent. One talkative friend of mine had his brand new car phone disconnected the day after his first bill arrived. He had no idea that the cure for his loneliness on the road could cost him a thousand dollars a month. I read about someone else who has lodged a complaint with the National Park Service about the use of cellular phones in the wilderness. It seems that his long-awaited trek to a landmark peak was ruined for him when a fellow traveler to the top whipped out his cordless and began describing the view to his children, who were apparently reluctant to be torn away from the television show they were watching at home.

The Park Service was sympathetic, since they have begun to receive more and more calls from hikers with cellular phones. Very few are genuine emergencies. The majority are from people who have gotten lost and want to be guided back to their cars by telephone, or who have developed painful blisters on their feet and want someone to come pick them up.

It is more and more difficult for us to choose silence when communication is possible. To let the telephone ring, to leave the e-mail unread, to unplug the fax machine—these amount to acts of social sabotage. To choose silence for even an hour, we must risk the loss of connection with other people, who may have a hard time understanding how anything could be more important to us than responding to them. We must also handle our own sense of anxiety. What if that is a call from the fire department? From the hospital? From someone who wants to invite me to dinner? For some of us, silence provokes so much internal chatter that it cancels itself out.

True silence is difficult to achieve, even at night when most of the world is asleep. A dedicated insomniac can count at least half a dozen engines running in the dark—the refrigerator, the water heater, the ice-maker, the furnace, the expressway noise that sounds like pounding surf at two in the morning, the distant roar of an airplane passing overhead. Depending on who you are, these sounds may be comforting. They mean everything is working. In the world of machines, silence signals malfunction. Remember the last time your electricity went off and all the sounds stopped, just like that?

Even our bodies are not silent. The composer John Cage has written about his visit to Harvard, where he spent some time in an anechoic chamber, a room without echoes. Inside, his perfect ears picked up two distinct sounds—one high and one low. When he described them to the engineer in charge, Cage learned that the high sound was his nervous system in operation, and the low one was his blood in circulation. "Until I die there will be sounds," he wrote afterward. "And they will continue following my death. One need not fear about the future of music."[1]

No wonder so many of us are ambivalent about silence. Silence may suggest tranquillity and awe, but it may also mean malfunction and death. Peace appeals to me, but not so much that I am ready to rest in peace. Making a little noise is how I remind myself that I am alive. It is how I exercise my superiority—over dirt, trees, and rocks—by mimicking the Creator who brought me into being with a word.

It is also how I act on my identity as a Christian. All who believe in the Word made flesh are inheritors of the Word. Hearing it and speaking it are how we keep it alive. When that Word fell silent on Golgotha—when, after a loud cry, both the high sound of his nervous system and the low sound of his beating heart stopped—the earth shook with grief. Rocks made the only sound they could, splitting open with small explosions that were their best version of tears. The veil in the temple was torn from top to bottom, with a sound of such ripping that those who heard it thought it was the sky. The whole inanimate world leapt in to fill that silence, while poor, dumb humanity stood speechless before the cross.

Later, after three days of complete quiet, the Word rose to break the silence. That familiar, beloved voice was once again heard on the earth, only briefly this time. Go, he said, *make disciples. Teach. Proclaim. Go.* Ready or not, it was the disciples' turn to speak. The Word had come back to entrust them with the Word. Then he disappeared for good.

His words did not disappear. They lingered in the air, still pulsing with power. All they needed to do their work was someone to speak them. If the disciples had any sense at all, they were scared to death to go near those words—not only because they recognized the power in them but also because they had revered the one who spoke them in the first place. Who was going to be the first to try on his words? They might as well dress up in his clothes and put his shoes on their feet. Who was going to pretend to be him?

Teach. Proclaim. Go. There was no way around it. The Word had willed them his words. And so the disciples entered the cloud of sacred speech. Peter was first, of course, but the others were not far behind. Before long they were all saying things they had never heard anyone but Jesus say before. Quoting him, they began to sound like him, and remarkable things happened around them when they did. People were healed, freed, fed, transformed. People called them gods and laid garlands at their feet, which gave them a chance to explain the difference between the Word and servants of the Word. But words remained the medium of relationship between the two. When the disciples spoke in the name of the Lord Jesus Christ, their words became acts. There was no vacuum between their saying and God's doing. When they spoke in the name of the Word made flesh, God came to earth all over again.

In this way, a certain kind of speech became definitive for Christians. The name they used for God set them apart from those who used other names. What they said they believed about God could get them killed, but saying it was so important to them that many of them willingly chose death over silence. As time went on, they compressed what they believed into a short version they could say together, and later they took their turns killing people who tried to say anything different about God.

"I believe" became the password for the Christian community. The creeds of the early church were recited before baptism and eucharist. They were the red flags waved in the faces of opponents, and they became even redder with the blood of those whose faith did not conform to them. The Word was described, defined, delimited by words, so that what Christians said became more decisive than anything they did.

Their job was to proclaim, which took them miles away from their Jewish forebears, whose job was to listen. The central Jewish declaration of faith is not "I believe," but "Hear, O Israel." The focus is on the ears, not the lips—on listening, not speaking. For the biblical Jew, God's name was unsayable. The only human being allowed to say it was the high priest in the temple in Jerusalem. Once a year, on Yom Kippur, he dared to utter God's name out loud as he pleaded for the life of the people. He knew that he risked his own life to do so, and it would never have occurred to him to compose a short, concise description of the G–D he encountered in the holy of holies.

Even now, some Christians have trouble listening to God. Many of us prefer to speak. Our corporate prayers are punctuated with phrases such as "Hear us, Lord" or "Lord, hear our prayer," as if the burden to listen were on God and not us. We name our concerns, giving God suggestions on what to do about them. What reversal of power might occur if we turned the process around, naming our concerns and asking God to tell us what to do about them? "Speak, Lord, for your servants are listening."

Sometimes I think we do all the talking because we are afraid God won't. Or, conversely, that God will. Either way, staying preoccupied with our own words seems a safer bet than opening ourselves up either to God's silence or God's speech, both of which have the power to undo us. In our own age, I believe God's silence is the more threatening, perhaps because it is the more frequently experienced of the two. Very few people come to see me because they want to discuss something God said to them last night. The large majority come because they cannot get God to say anything at all. They have asked as sincerely as they know how for answers, for guidance, for peace, but they are still missing those things. They want me to tell them what they have done wrong. They have heard me talk about God on Sundays and they hope they can make use of my connections. Perhaps I know a special technique they can try or—better yet—perhaps I can lend my own weight to the cause, adding the poundage of my prayers to theirs in an effort to force some sound from God.

Their wish to hear God speak is not unfounded. The Bible they read portrays a God who not only speaks but who also acts. Right there on the page, the faithful receive what they ask for: children, manna, land, health. By implication, those who do not receive are not faithful. They are not right with God. If they were, God would speak to them. "For everyone who asks receives, and everyone who searches finds, and for everyone who knocks, the door will be opened" (Luke 11:10).

This is the condemnation that hangs over the silence of God, as if that silence could mean only one thing. Meanwhile, scripture is full of silences, both human and divine, that mean not one but many different things.

The phrase *hester panim*, the hiding of the face, occurs more than thirty times in the Hebrew Bible in reference to God.[2] The major prophets all use it. So do the psalmists (10:11, 13:1, 30:7, 44:24, 88:14) and the writer of Deuteronomy. In Deuteronomy 32, after Moses has finished writing down the words of the law "to the very end," God predicts that all in all it will not do much good—that people being people, it will not be long before they are dancing with cows again. So Moses writes a warning song and sings it to the whole assembly of Israel, reminding them what will happen when they do. "I will hide my face from them," God says in that song, "I will see what their end will be" (32:20). *Memorize this*, Moses says to the people. When they can no longer remember the sound of God's voice, he wants them to know why.

Hebrew scholar Richard Elliott Friedman has written a book called *The Disappearance of God*, in which he chronicles divine recession in the Hebrew Bible. Working his way from Genesis to the minor prophets, he paints a portrait of God that fades as he goes. Divine features that were distinct at the beginning of the story grow blurry as God withdraws, stepping back from human beings so that they have room to step forward.

After Babel, Friedman says, God was never again made visible to all humankind.[3] The people of Israel were extended special privileges that lasted throughout their forty years in the wilderness, but once Moses saw God's backside on Mount Sinai, the period of visible, audible encounters with God began to come to an end. After the delivery of the commandments, God never spoke directly to the people again. Moses the mediator wore a veil. The ark of the covenant was placed inside a tent. When Moses died, there was no one left on earth who had actually laid eyes on God.

As the biblical story goes on, God continues to retreat. According to Friedman, the last person to whom God was said to have been "revealed" was Samuel in the temple at Shiloh (1 Samuel 3:21). The last person to whom God was said to have "appeared" was Solomon—once at Gibeon and again when the king finished building the temple in Jerusalem (1 Kings 3:5, 9:2).[4] After that, the verb is retired in reference to God. The people have prophets, kings, and temples to preoccupy them. Why do they need God?

The last public miracle recorded in the Hebrew Bible was the spectacle on Mount Carmel (1 Kings 18). Hundreds of people watched as God helped

Elijah single-handedly whip the prophets of Baal, but after that God assumed a lower profile, working miracles for smaller and smaller audiences. Even angels got scarce: there is no evidence they tended to anyone after Elijah. Gradually, the prophetic experience of God became one of visions and dreams. From Hezekiah on, the world described in the Hebrew Bible was one from which God had largely retired, leaving humans to interact with other humans. The acts of God were over. The remembered words of God took their place. The world was no longer a place where seas split and snakes talked, but one in which human relationship to the divine was largely a matter of personal belief.[5]

This is the world into which Jesus was born—the clearest revelation of God's presence on earth since Sinai. In Jesus, God was once again made both audible and visible. Miracles followed him around. Angels attended his birth and ministered to him in the wilderness. Wind and water did what he said. In him, the Word of God was translated back into the acts of God. He was, for many people, their dream of God come true.

But not everyone could see and hear God in him. His miracles tended to be intimate ones. They did not change the political destiny of the people, as Moses' had, nor bring Israel's oppressors to their knees. With a few exceptions, he saved people's lives one at a time as he laid hands on their sick heads, rubbed mud on their blind eyes, evicted their demons with a few loud words from his lips.

If people did not hear God in him they were pretty much out of luck, because God did not say all that much apart from him. The synoptic gospels agree that it happened twice—once at the River Jordan and once on the Mount of Transfiguration. "This is my Son, my Beloved. Listen to him." John's gospel mentions a third time during the last week of Jesus' life, but that incident highlights the problem. When a voice from heaven addressed Jesus, some standing there heard it and said that it was thunder (John 12:29). There is always another explanation. The point, as Fred

Craddock has said, is that the voice of God in Jesus was not a shout. In him, the revelation of God comes to us as a whisper.[6] In order to catch it, we must hush, lean forward, and trust that what we hear is the voice of God.

Whatever you think of this chronology, it is hard to deny that the mode of God's revelation has changed over the course of time. Apart from reports of the sun spinning in the sky at Medugorje or the Virgin Mary appearing in a backyard in Conyers, Georgia, there are not many corporate visions of God anymore. Conclusive miracles are hard to come by, and few of us would enter a contest of faith like Elijah's, in which our success depended on getting God to spit fire in front of hundreds of people. Times have changed. Our experience of God has changed, and it is not all God's fault.

Many people pray for an encounter with the living God. Those whose prayers are answered rarely ask for the same thing twice. Even if all they got was a slight blast of God's exhaust, they can usually tell you what the Bible means by "the fear of the Lord." They know better than to fool around with divine presence. They would be safer splitting atoms. Someday I would like to hear a debate between them and some other religious people I know about whether or not human beings are constitutionally able to encounter God without turning to ash on the spot.

The people of Israel did not think so. If I were to choose the moment when our real problems with God began, I would not choose the one in the garden of Eden, nor the one that led to the flood, nor the one that resulted in the tower of Babel. I would choose the moment right after God spoke the ten commandments at Sinai. According to the book of Exodus, all the people were there. Not one of them missed it: God's own voice, with thunder in it and lightning cracking all around; the sound of a trumpet none of them knew how to play, with notes that made their scalps crawl; the mountain itself, smoking like a kiln, shaking so violently that the ground slid beneath their feet.

It was an encounter with the living God, and in about five seconds they decided they had had enough. Turning to Moses, they said, "You speak to us, and we will listen; but do not let God speak to us, or we will die" (Exodus 20:19). They were not up to a direct encounter. They wanted a mediator, and in that moment the ministry was born—an opening for someone to stand between the people and God, someone to take the heat, veil the light, buffer the noise, deliver the message in a human voice, so the people could hear it without fainting from fear.

At their request, God never spoke to all the people again. Secondary speech replaced primary speech. The pillar of fire and cloud that led the people through the wilderness gave way to a tabernacle they could carry around with them. The hot lava of God's voice cooled into the six hundred thirteen commandments of the law. In time, books, clergy, and institutions of worship would become substitutes for the presence of the living God, and that would suit almost everyone just fine. In George Steiner's apt phrase, "We seek the immunities of indirection." We welcome those "who can domesticate, who can secularize the mystery and summons of creation."[7]

We are cowards, in other words. We have good reason to be. Just ask Father Abraham. Long before the people asked to be delivered from God's voice at Sinai, Abraham had his own encounter with that voice in the land of Moriah. He and God had been in conversation for a quarter of a century by then. God had moved him and Sarah from Haran to Hebron with a whole lot of stops in between. God had dickered with him over the fate of Sodom, and had given him advice on the strife between the mothers of his children. God had made promises to him and begun to deliver on them. Abraham and Sarah had a son, Isaac, whom they loved. He was the only fruit that had dropped from their old, intertwined trees. He was the first star in their sky, a sky God had promised to fill with their descendants. He was precious to them.

Which was why it was such a shock for Abraham to hear God's familiar voice telling him to set Isaac on fire. The same voice that had said, "Your wife Sarah shall bear you a son, and you shall name him Isaac," now said, "Take your son, your only son Isaac, whom you love, and go to the land of Moriah, and offer him there as a burnt offering on one of the mountains that I shall show you" (Genesis 22:2). And that was all God said. There was no word from the Lord as Abraham rose the next morning to chop firewood in the dark, burying his ax in the grain again and again. God was silent as Abraham saddled his donkey and went to wake his servants and his child. God was silent as the small party set out, and silent for the three days it took them to find the place.

When they got there, the only voice Abraham heard was his own. "Stay here with the donkey," he told his servants. "The boy and I will go over there; we will worship, and then we will come back to you." It was a lie, but what was he to do? Let Isaac hear what God had said or protect the boy from the knowledge of God? Abraham protected him, to the point of assuring his son when he asked that God would provide a lamb for the burnt offering.

But when they came to the place that God had shown him, there was no lamb in sight. There was also no word from the Lord. The only sound was Abraham's loud breath as he squatted to lift the stones for the altar. Isaac too was silent as he watched his father work, first making a table out of the rocks, then laying the firewood on top of the rocks. Abraham laid it this way and he laid it that way, or at least that was what he seemed to be doing. What he was really doing was listening—listening so hard it made his head hurt and his chest ache, fooling around with the rocks and the wood until he could find no more reasons to stall. God was not going to speak. Abraham could protect his son no longer.

He turned to the boy, and I am glad that scripture spares us the details. According to Genesis, there was no struggle, no screaming. Abraham did not have to chase his son and tackle him. He did not have to force the boy's skinny arms behind his back and carry him shrieking toward the furnace. "He bound his son Isaac, and laid him on the altar, on top of the wood." That is all it says, but you have to wonder why it was so easy. Had the boy fainted? Had his father knocked him out?

"Then Abraham reached out his hand and took the knife to kill his son."

Never in the history of the world, I think, had there been such a silence. No one said a word. Not Abraham. Not Isaac. Not God. It was the knife's turn to speak, until an angel cleared its throat: "Abraham," it said, "Abraham!"

And Abraham said, "Here I am." It was the word he had been waiting for. His son was spared. He had passed the test, but Abraham never talked to God again. In the years that were left to him, he spoke *about* God often enough, but he never again spoke *to* God, and God respected the silence. Their conversation was over. Abraham's reward for obeying God's voice was never to have to hear it again.[8]

According to the Midrash, the encounter on Mount Moriah was so overwhelming that Isaac was blinded by it and Abraham became deaf, while Sarah died of grief. If this is the price of direct encounter with God, is it any wonder that human beings pulled away? The resistance of the prophets is legendary. "O my Lord, please send someone else," Moses said to the God of the burning bush (Exodus 4:13). Isaiah's excuse was that he was unclean, and Jeremiah's that he was too young.

Ezekiel kept his lips pressed firmly together until God shoved a scroll through them. When he still refused to speak, God put a divine lock on his lips. "I will make your tongue cling to the roof of your mouth, so that you shall be speechless," God said to him in the third chapter of his book, and it was not until the thirty-third chapter that the ban was lifted (33:22). But at least Ezekiel remained in the presence of God. Jonah did his best to flee it, going west when God said to go east, as if he could actually turn his back on God.

These people knew what it meant to be bearers of God's word. That word was a hot coal, a potter's fist, a hungry bear in the night. One spoke it at risk of one's life—not only because of the reaction it might provoke but also because of its origin. To put God's word into a human mouth was to push flesh to its limit. It was like carrying nitroglycerin around in a crystal goblet. It was like describing the Pleiades over a tin can telephone. And yet people did it, because God commanded them. People still do it, although I am not sure we reckon it a risk anymore.

When we speak of God, we do not sound so much like people with fire shut up in our bones as we do like people who are blowing on gray coals, hunting around between breaths for anything we can toss on top of them that might keep them from going out altogether. The landscape has been picked pretty clean by now. We can lay our hands on so little that many of us have resorted to secondhand fuel, subscribing to magazines full of homiletical kindling that has already been used elsewhere. It works about as well as those pressed wood-fiber logs you can buy at the grocery store. It keeps the fire going, but it neither looks nor smells like the real thing.

Where has the Firemaker gone? Where is the God of the burning bush, the God in the pillar of fire and cloud, the God who personally incinerated one whole bull in the contest on Mount Carmel, although the altar had been soaked with twelve jars of water?

The obvious answer is that we have turned away. From our fright at the foot of Mount Sinai to our uneasy acquaintance with the patriarchs and prophets, plenty of us have concluded that we are not up to direct encounter with God. We want it but we don't want it. We want to be warmed, not burned, except where God is concerned there is no such thing as safe fire. Safe fire is our own invention. It is what we preach to people who, like us, would rather be bored than scared.

And yet there is scriptural evidence that God has turned away from us as well. The silence has two sides. In third Isaiah, God is very forthright about turning away from the people. "Why do we fast, but you do not see?" they complain. "Why humble ourselves, but you do not notice?" (58:3). It is God's absence that has provoked their questions—a creative hiding of the divine face that has brought the people out of their own hiding. Once God has their attention, they get their answer: it is not God's absence from them that is the problem but their absence from God. They have substituted liturgy for justice. They have fasted without offering their untouched food to the hungry. They have put on their sackcloth and ashes without removing the yoke from the neck of the oppressed. God is silent because they do not speak God's language. But it took God's silence to teach them that.

This game of divine hide and seek is part of God's pedagogy in Isaiah, which makes silence a vital component of God's speech. Tragically, the game often backfires. Like restless children easily distracted, the people seek God for a little while and then go off to make mud pies, without ever discovering God's hiding place.

"I was ready to be sought out by those who did not ask," God laments, "to be found by those who did not seek me. I said, 'Here I am, here I am,' to a nation that did not call on my name. I held out my hands all day long to a rebellious people" (Isaiah 65:1-2a).

In the book of Job, God gets even. "I cry to you and you do not answer me," Job says late in his soliloquy before God. "I stand, and you merely look at me" (Job 30:20). There may be no other piece of biblical literature that has appealed to as wide an audience of believers and unbelievers alike. Writers as diverse as Gustavo Gutierrez and William Safire have dedicated whole volumes to Job, and Job's protest remains one of the most eloquent complaints we have against a God who does not respond when we call.

I am told that Virginia Woolf once wrote a friend, "I read the Book of Job last night—I don't think God comes well out of it." More important for those of us who preach, neither do Job's friends. They do their best work at the beginning, before they ever open their mouths. For seven days and seven nights they sit on the ground with Job, struck as dumb as he is by the enormity of his suffering. But their compassion for him dissolves once he starts railing at God. His outrage loosens their tongues. They tell him he must have done something to deserve it all, since God does not make mistakes. Instead of defending their friend against God, they defend God against their friend. *God is just*, they tell him. *Therefore you must be guilty*.

Only Job knows he is not guilty, and so does God. What is happening to him defies all human logic, which his friends cannot stand, so they cope with Job's pain by coming up with pious theories to explain it. The more he suffers, the more they talk, until Job cannot take it anymore. "What you know, I also know," he reminds them. "I am not inferior to you. But I would speak to the Almighty, and I desire to argue my case with God. As for you, you whitewash with lies; all of you are worthless physicians. If you would only keep silent, that would be your wisdom!" (13:2-5).

Job prefers God's silence to the explanations of his friends. In their ministerial anxiety, they are like flies buzzing around him on his dung heap. If they would just shut up, he could take his case to the Source instead of wasting his energy on the intermediaries. They are in his way. They are in God's way. They are trying to insert themselves between the silence of God and the one for whom the silence is intended, and in the end their interpretations are more painful to Job than the silence itself. He can accept that God may not be speaking to him. What he cannot accept is that these self-appointed deputies should presume to speak in God's place.[9]

"Let me have silence, and I will speak," he roars at them, "and let come on me what may. I will take my flesh in my teeth, and put my life in my hand." And then, in the famous line that has been translated so divergently, "See, he will kill me; I have no hope; but I will defend my ways to his face" (13:13-15).

God does not kill Job. Instead, God addresses him at last. The divine rebuttal goes on for four whole chapters, in fact, but God never does answer Job's question. Job's question was about justice. God's answer is about omnipotence, and as far as I know that is the only reliable answer human beings have ever gotten about why things happen the way they do. God only knows. And we are not God.

When the dust settles, Job is strangely pacified. In his last, short speech to God Job admits, "I have spoken of the unspeakable and tried to grasp the infinite. I had heard of you with my ears; but now my eyes have seen you. Therefore, I will be quiet, comforted that I am dust."[10] Why quiet, since he never got an answer, and why comforted that he is dust? Because Job, of all people, lured God out of hiding. He saw God face to face—*panim* to *panim*—and lived to tell the tale.

His friends, meanwhile, are chastised by the God they worked so hard to defend. In the same way that Job prefers God's silence to their chatter, God prefers Job's outrage to their preaching. "My wrath is kindled against you and against your two friends," God says to Eliphaz the Temanite, "for you have not spoken of me what is right, as my servant Job has" (42:7).

I am thinking of the same man I mentioned earlier, who lost his voice when his wife died. He says that while he is grateful to everyone who ministered to him, the people he remembers best are the ones who had no words, no answers. He calls them "the silent comforters," and suspects that they were truer mediators of God than the visitors who tried to staunch his grief with words. As a preacher, he wonders what this means. Is

God more at home in silence than in word? Is the moment of most profound silence the moment of God's most profound presence? "I don't know," he answers himself, "but at my wife's bedside, where words were hollow and cries powerless, the strongest, most powerful reality was silence."

It is no coincidence, I think, that so much of the literature on the silence of God has been written by Jews. *The Exile of the Word: From the Silence of the Bible to the Silence of Auschwitz* by Andre Neher. *The Disappearance of God* by Richard Elliott Friedman. *In Speech and In Silence: The Jewish Quest for God* by David Wolpe. *The Eclipse of God* by Martin Buber. Each of these writers is a Holocaust survivor, even if he never set foot in a camp. Each writes with the knowledge that the sky can grow dark with smoke from burning human bodies without so much as a whimper from God.

For some survivors, this knowledge has resulted in a relinquishment of God. For these particular writers, it has resulted more in what I would call a relinquishment of certain language about God. As Buber makes clear, a divine eclipse does not mean that God is dead, as rumor had it in the sixties. "An eclipse of the sun is something that occurs between the sun and our eyes," he explains, "not in the sun itself."[11] He goes on to suggest that what blocks the sun from our eyes is the radical subjectivism of our age, in which our knowledge of God is limited by our language. As "pure Thouness," he says, God is not objectifiable. "Words serve only as mute gestures pointing to the irreducible, ineffable dimension where God subsists."[12]

If he is right, as I believe he is, then what about the Word made flesh? If God is more present in silence than in words, if our best words cannot aspire to more than pointing toward the God who is beyond them, then what are we to make of the Incarnate Word? Jesus could have come to us as the Incarnate Silence, after all, or as the Incarnate Mystery. That he was revealed to John as the Incarnate Word seems to assert the sayability of God in a whole new way. In Jesus, the silent God found a voice. In Jesus, the irreducible God took on a human body. And those of us who believe it assume responsibility for proclaiming it so that others might believe it too. Our relationship to the Word requires us to use words. Our vocation is not only to do what the Word told us to do but also to say what the Word told us to say, until the whole world is transformed by the news.

As I said earlier, this has had the effect of making Christianity an overly talkative religion, but the truth is that silence plays as central a role in Christian scripture as in Hebrew. In each of the gospels, the Word comes forth from silence. For John, it is the silence at the beginning of creation. For Luke, it is the silence of poor old Zechariah, struck dumb by the angel Gabriel for doubting that Elizabeth would bear a child. For Matthew, it is the awkward silence between Joseph and Mary when she tells him her prenuptial news, and for Mark it is the voice of one crying in the wilderness—the long-forgotten voice of prophecy puncturing the silence of the desert and of time.

Silence was the backdrop against which the Word began to be heard. While Jesus stood in the wings, John the Baptist prepared the way, using such ferocious language that many must have expected a fire-breathing messiah to drop from the sky. Instead it was Jesus who came among them, making so little noise that even John did not know who he was at first. Even when he spoke, Jesus created silence. Many of his sayings were so cryptic that no response was possible, while others were so offensive that replies were withheld. "Love your enemies, do good to those who hate you, bless those who curse you, pray for those who abuse you" (Luke 6:27-28). Any questions?

He was a genius storyteller, with a gift for surprise endings that left his listeners shaking their heads. He almost never wrapped things up for them. He did not make the elder brother go into the house to welcome his baby brother home. He made no apology for the farm manager who paid the latecomers as much as the early risers, nor did he say anything in defense of the underdressed wedding guest who was thrown into outer darkness by the king's thugs. He did not mess up the silence in his stories by supplying them with morals. He left the problems in them, so that his listeners could experience the silence for themselves.

He also did not star in his own stories. He never once said, "An interesting thing happened to me on my way here this morning…." It was almost impossible to get him to talk about himself, except in terms of who he was not or what he was about to lose. When people sought answers from him, he asked them questions instead, creating a silence that only they could fill. "Teacher, what must I do to inherit eternal life?" "What is written in the law? What do you read there?" (Luke 10:25-26).

His preaching was full of such questions, which left great pockets of silence in his proclamation. "Is not life more than food, and the body more than clothing?" (Matthew 6:25). "Can a blind person guide a blind person? Will not both fall into a pit?" (Luke 6:39). "Is there anyone among you who, if your child asks for bread, will give a stone?" (Matthew 7:9). Over and over, he reached out to those who looked to him for answers and turned them around to look at the world instead—at sibling rivalries and unjust labor practices, at miffed royalty and mugged travelers—not to dodge his listeners' search for meaning but to enroll them in the making of it. His silence gave them room to speak, and better yet, to act. His restraint guaranteed their freedom, which they might or might not use to seek God. The choice was theirs, as it remains ours.[13]

This reserve set Jesus apart from his predecessors. In him, God spoke so softly that not everyone heard. What a change from the old days in the wilderness, when God's voice was enough to make the whole people of Israel beg for mercy! What had changed? God's voice or human ears? Most people I ask say *we* are to blame, that if we cannot hear God's voice it is because we are not listening.

But even if that is true most of the time, it is not true all of the time. The death of Jesus taught us that. From the moment he came down from the mount of the Transfiguration, the memory of God's voice was all he had left. He prayed to hear it again in the garden of Gethsemane, but the only voice he heard there was his own. He was arrested, tried, and convicted without so much as a sigh from heaven. From the cross, he pleaded for a word, any word, from the God he could no longer hear. He asked for bread and got a stone. Finally, in the most profound silence of his life, he died, believing himself forsaken by God.

Will anyone suggest that he simply was not listening? I do not think so. In the silence surrounding his death, Jesus became the best possible companion for those whose prayers are not answered, who would give anything just to hear God call them by name. Him too. He wanted that too, and he did not get it. What he got, instead, was a fathomless silence in which to cry out. Forever after, everyone who has heard him bellow into it has had to wonder: Is that the voice of God?

There is a story from the Sufi tradition about a man who cried, "Allah! Allah!" until his lips became sweet with the sound. A skeptic who heard him said, "Well! I have heard you calling out, but where is the answer to your prayer? Have you ever gotten a response?" The man had no answer to that. Sadly, he abandoned his prayers and went to sleep. In his dreams he saw Khazir, the soul guide, walking toward him through a garden.

"Why did you stop praising?" the saint asked him. "Because I never heard anything back," the man said. "This longing you voice *is* the return message," Khazir told him.

> The grief you cry out from
> draws you toward union.
>
> Your pure sadness
> that wants help
> is the secret cup.
>
> Listen to the moan of a dog
>   for its master.
> That whining is the connection.
>
> There are love dogs
> no one knows the names of.
>
> Give your life
> to be one of them.[14]

Only an idol always answers. The God who keeps silence, even when God's own flesh and blood is begging for a word, is the God beyond anyone's control. An answer will come, but not until the silence is complete. And even then, the answer will be given in silence. With the cross and the empty tomb, God has provided us with two events that defy all our efforts to domesticate them. Before them, and before the God who is present in them, our most eloquent words turn to dust. In the last chapter I want to talk about how we may approach this God with all due respect, proclaiming the Word without violating the silence, by speaking with restraint.

Endnotes

1. John Cage, *Silence: Lectures and Writings by John Cage* (Middletown, Conn.: Wesleyan University Press, 1973), 8.
2. Richard Elliott Friedman, *The Disappearance of God: A Divine Mystery* (Boston: Little, Brown and Company, 1995), 69. This book has been reissued under the title *The Hidden Face of God*.
3. *Ibid.*, 8.

4. *Ibid.*, 20.

5. *Ibid.*, 77.

6. Fred B. Craddock, *Preaching* (Nashville: Abingdon Press, 1985), 57.

7. George Steiner, *Real Presences* (Chicago: The University of Chicago Press, 1989), 39.

8. Andre Neher, *The Exile of the Word: From the Silence of the Bible to the Silence of Auschwitz* (Philadelphia: The Jewish Publication Society of America, 5741/1981), 178.

9. *Ibid.*, 32, 35.

10. Stephen Mitchell, *The Book of Job* (San Francisco: North Point Press, 1979), 88.

11. Martin Buber, *The Eclipse of God: Studies in the Relation Between Religion and Philosophy* (Atlantic Highlands, N.J.: Humanities Press International, Inc., 1988), 23.

12. *Ibid.*, xiii.

13. I am grateful to James Breech, author of *The Silence of Jesus: The Authentic Voice of the Historical Man* (Philadelphia: Fortress Press, 1983), for informing my thinking about the silence of Jesus.

14. This story combines two tellings of it: one from A. J. Arberry's *Tales from the Masnavi* and the other from Coleman Barks's translation of Rumi. The last eleven lines of verse come from the poem "Love Dogs" in *The Essential Rumi*,

translated by Coleman Barks with John Moyne, A. J. Arberry, and Reynold Nicholson (SanFrancisco: Harper, 1995), 155.

~ THREE ~

Restraint

$\mathcal{M}$ost of us have been taught that we should abandon restraint in the preaching of God's word. For plenty of us, the perfect preacher is someone who stands in the pulpit radiating confidence—someone so grounded in Holy Scripture, so guided by the Holy Spirit that flames seem to shoot from the mouth and every word reverberates with God's own *Amen.* There is no doubt in this picture, no struggle for speech. Restraint would ruin it. Restraint would sound like cowardice, or stinginess. In a time of famine, one should open all the storehouses and bring out all the food, right? One should open all the faucets and let the healing waters flow.

Well, maybe. And maybe not. Last year I complained in writing to a friend that I was not sure people even listened to sermons anymore. She wrote back, "I do think people are trying to listen and that preaching *does* matter. In fact, I think the vast majority of people are sitting in the pews with parched lips. They are so thirsty that they have lost their ability to listen, to speak, or to think. But one big gulp of Gatorade is not the answer. They will drown. Their thirst is so great that it requires a series of sips much like parched fields require a series of gentle rains."

Her words, in combination with my reading of God's silence in the Bible, give me courage to explore the practice of restraint in preaching—not as a deliberate withholding of God's word nor, I hope, as a rationale for my own reticence, but as a sober reaching for more reverence in the act of public speaking about God. Any way you look at it, that act is a foolhardy thing to do. Who will volunteer to conduct lightning from heaven to earth? Who will offer a guided tour through the beating heart of God? People more faithful than we have gotten killed doing things like that, and yet plenty of us climb into pulpits Sunday after Sunday with no more sense of danger than if we were climbing into our cars to go fetch a quart of milk. We do not even put our seat belts on. Why? Because we do not expect anything serious to happen, any more than our congregations do.

Restraint

When Blaise Pascal died in 1662, his servant found a scrap of paper hidden in the lining of his coat. It turned out to be a testimony of something that had happened eight years earlier, which Pascal had written down and kept close to his heart. Here is what it said:

> In the year of Grace, 1654,
> On Monday, 23rd of November,
>   Feast of St. Clement, Pope and Martyr,
>   and of others in the Martyrology,
> Vigil of Saint Chrysogonus,
>   martyr and others,
> From about half past ten in the evening
> until about half past twelve
>   FIRE
> God of Abraham, God of Isaac,
>   God of Jacob
> not of the philosophers and scholars.
> Certitude. Certitude. Feeling. Joy. Peace.
> God of Jesus Christ.[1]

Whatever happened to him that Monday night, FIRE was all he could say about it. For two whole hours, nothing but FIRE—not the fire of philosophers and scholars but the fire of God, unmediated, undeniable, and finally unsayable, although the few words Pascal plucked out of the flames have more power in them than five pages of precise description. These were the words he carried next to his heart. In his published work he managed complete sentences, such as this one from his *Pensées*: "Every religion which does not affirm that God is hidden," he wrote, "is not true."[2]

On the face of it, God's hiddenness, like God's silence, would seem to threaten the whole enterprise of religion, but in fact the opposite is true. If God were readily accessible to people who could safely make use of that access, then religion would become obsolete. Oh, some hymns and prayers might survive, but there would be no further need for clergy, sacraments, or systems of belief. People could simply go straight to the source. Instead they come to us, which means that our livelihood as preachers depends as much on God's hiddenness as it does on God's presence. In a world of professionals, we are the religious experts, and God's silence is the problem we are hired to solve. Listen to Jelaluddin Rumi, mystic poet of thirteenth-century Persia:

> I've said before that every craftsman
> searches for what's not there
> to practice his craft.
> A builder looks for the rotten hole
> where the roof caved in. A water carrier
> picks the empty pot. A carpenter
> stops at the house with no door.
>
> Workers rush toward some hint
> of emptiness, which they then
> start to fill. Their hope, though,
> is for emptiness, so don't think
> you must avoid it. It contains
> what you need![3]

These verses describe the paradox all preachers must learn to navigate: namely, that our speech exists in tension with God's silence. Our job is to speak. It was not God who named the animals, after all, but Adam. One by one God set the creatures down in front of him to see what he would call them. The making belonged to God, but the speaking belonged to Adam and soon to Eve as well, who turned out to be quite a daring conversationalist.

We have been given the same privilege in our own time, only the subject of our speech is much more elusive than anything Adam and Eve faced. One moment it looks like a lion and the next like a lamb. One moment it looks like a dove fanning the sun with its white wings and the next like an eagle bearing down on its prey. Every saying demands an unsaying: our God is like this, yet not like this; resembling that, but then again not. Our God is hidden not behind a wall but behind a translucent veil. We see, only dimly, and as the focus of our scrutiny goes on morphing before our eyes, we must finally make peace with the incompleteness of our saying, which draws near to but cannot penetrate the silence of God's pure being.

Language is the deck of cards we have been given to name our experience. There are hundreds of games we can play with it, but in the end there are only fifty-two cards. We cannot say anything with five aces in it, or win an argument that calls for three red queens. There are limits to our language, and while most of the time fifty-two cards seem entirely too few, the truth is that more would ruin the game. Because we are limited in what we can say, we know what it is to come to the end of speech—to come to the very edge of language—and to gaze slack-jawed at what still lies beyond. If you have ever stood on a high cliff over the sea and felt that strange, frightening pull toward the brink, then you know what I mean. There is a human fascination with limits that is both holy and chastening all at the same time.

Without limits, we would have no feel for the infinite. Without limits, we would be freed from our longing for what lies beyond. It is precisely our inability to say God that teaches us who God is. When we run out of words, we are very near the God whose name is unsayable. The fact that we cannot say it, however, does not mean we may stop trying. The trying is essential to our humanity. It is how we push language to the limit so that we may listen to it as it falls, exploding into scripture, sonnet, story, song. All these may fail in the end to name the living God, but they fail like shooting stars.

In one of his books, Martin Buber remembers being the house guest of a philosophy professor who offered him a bed and the use of a study while Buber was lecturing in town. One morning Buber rose early to read the proofs of his latest book which, in its preface, contained the closest thing he had ever written to a statement of faith. Going down to the study that had been offered him, he was surprised to find his host already sitting there in the early morning light. The man asked Buber what he had in his hand and, when he found out, asked Buber to read it to him.

Buber agreed, but was not encouraged by the look of alarm that spread over his host's face as he read what he had written. Afterward the old philosopher said, "How can you bring yourself to say 'God' time after time? How can you expect that your readers will take the word in the sense in which you wish it to be taken? What you mean by the name of God is something above all human grasp and comprehension, but in speaking about it you have lowered it to human conceptualization." The man went on to mourn all the innocent blood that had been shed in that name, all the injustice it had been used to cover. "When I hear the highest called 'God,'" he said, "it sometimes seems almost blasphemous."

Buber says the two men just sat there in silence for a while, each of them regarding the other. Then Buber said he agreed with the man. The word "God" was the most heavy-laden of all human words. There was no other word that had become so soiled, so mutilated. That was the reason he could not abandon it. He understood, he said, why "some suggest we should remain silent about the 'last things' for a time in order that the misused words may be redeemed! But they are not to be redeemed *thus*. We cannot cleanse the word 'God' and we cannot make it whole; but, defiled and mutilated as it is, we can raise it from the ground and set it over an hour of great care."[4]

This rescue effort calls for a delicate touch. In order to participate in it, we need first of all to remember that it is not God we are rescuing but ourselves. While our trespasses on God's name and being may not escape divine notice, we are the ones who are damaged by them. By thoughtlessly lumbering over the limits set for us, we have driven God further away from us. By using God's name to endorse our own products, we have lost the ability to distinguish between God's voice and our own. We are the losers here, and the remedy for having said too much already is not to say more. The rescue effort begins with saying less.

In his book *The Silence of Jesus*, James Breech recalls going to hear W. H. Auden read some of his poetry at Princeton years ago. The lecture hall was jammed, he says, with hundreds of people all chattering with excitement. When the old man finally came out on the stage to read, he read in a voice so soft that even the microphone did not help. People immediately began whispering to each other what they thought Auden had said until the poet himself could no longer be heard. His would-be interpreters had drowned him out. What Breech learned that night, he says, is that "if we want to hear what a speaker is saying while others are talking, even though they are trying to be helpful, their voices distract our attention and interfere with our listening. In order for the speaker's own voice to be heard, the go-betweens must be silent."[5]

When the poet happens to be God, this advice takes on special significance. Among Christians, perhaps only Quakers have taken it entirely to heart, but even if the rest of us go-betweens were to sit in church with duct tape on our mouths, the difference is this: the space behind the microphone would remain empty. There would be no one on the stage, because God does not show up to read God's own poetry. God has delegated that job. If the poems are to be heard, then someone must dare to climb up on the stage, open the book, and read. But not without listening first—listening for the voice of the author—so that the reading is true.

I am wondering about the place of listening in a preacher's life. Where do you go to listen for God's silence and God's speech? Who taught you to do that and whom have you taught to do the same thing? It is a dying art, which may be a large part of our language difficulties these days. Silence and speech define each other. One is the inhale. The other is the exhale. Like prayer and proclamation, they perfect each other, although in our day their ecology is seriously out of whack.

"There is more silence in one person than can be used in a single human life," writes Max Picard, who laments a world drowning in a downpour of noise. When he looks around for some means of survival, he says that sometimes a cathedral looks to him like a great ark into which all creation is being gathered to save it from the flood of noise.[6]

It is a lovely image. Outside, the air is dense with horns, with sirens, with the hiss and rumble of city buses. Drivers listen to loud car radios and pedestrians shout into their cell phones, while the buzz of a dozen talk shows spills through open living room windows and puddles in the street. A corporate helicopter whup-whup-whups overhead, brakes screech, a policeman yells through a loudspeaker at a bicycle thief.

Most people are so used to wading through the noise that they do not even notice how deep it has gotten. If someone were to tell them it was about to close over their heads they would not even be able to hear the warning, but a few of them have noticed what is happening. They are the ones walking up the steps of the cathedral, toward the promise of silence. The steps are littered with beepers, with telephones, with Walkman radios and portable CD players. The appliances crunch underfoot as people walk over them. A few skitter back down the steps into the street.

There are people on those steps but there are animals too (this is an ark, remember?)—carriage horses who have had it up to here with taxis, dogs tired of barking at strange noises in the night, parrots who do not want to learn any more clever human phrases, and a whole herd of escapees from the circus who have grown weary of applause. With all this noise still raining down on them, they step into the silence of the cathedral.

Inside, it is another world. It is so quiet they can hear one another breathing. It is so quiet they can hear the candles burning, the flowers spilling their sweet scent. There is no question where all that silence is coming from. It is rolling toward them from the altar, the still center of the ark, where it is so quiet they can hear Someone Else think.

I don't know if you can see your own church this way, but if you can then you know there is work to do. As chaplains on this ark, what is our responsibility toward silence? What should we teach our children about it? How can we commend it to our young people, for whom noise is as addictive as any drug? And what shall we say about it to our old people, who may have far too much silence in their lives? Whatever there is to say, no one will listen to us unless we can offer them evidence of our own relationship to silence. If we simply dip our cups into the noisy torrent of the world and serve it up with a little theological parsley on top, people will learn to look elsewhere for food. At the very least, we owe them words we have dug up with our own hands, words we have brought back from our own encounter with the silence. Our authority to speak is rooted in our ability to remain silent.

In the context of homiletics, this produces a real oxymoron. How does one preach silence? More to the point, how does one preach without profaning God's silence, without getting between that silence and those for whom it is intended?

I have several suggestions for those of us who have volunteered for the job. They are not authoritative, by any means, any more than they are complete. I expect to spend the rest of my life learning about the proper relationship between human speech and the silence of God. But for purposes of discussion, I want to talk about homiletical restraint in terms of *economy*, *courtesy*, and *reverence* in the language we use.

First, I suppose I should settle the question of whom I believe we are addressing when we talk about God. In the Episcopal Church, we used to answer that question by turning round and round all Sunday morning long. First we faced the people for the opening sentences, then we faced the altar for the collect for purity. We turned around for the proclamation of the word and back again for the Nicene Creed. We faced the people for the absolution, faced the altar for the Great Thanksgiving. Around and around we went, speaking God's word to the people, speaking the people's words to God.

We stopped doing that, for the most part, in the seventies, when we pulled the altars out from the wall and stood behind them to face the people. But I think we are still doing that inside, whether we are preaching or leading worship—we are turning round and round, only our voices carry both ways. When we address God, the people are listening. When we address the people, God is listening. We serve them both, although we are people ourselves. We listen to both, although it is God who has the last word.

Sometimes I think we resemble matchmakers more than anything else. Turning one way, we carry the longings of the human heart to God. *Do you love us? Do you care?* Turning the other way, we bring back the answer. *The reason you do not know is that you have never been loved like this before. If you let me, I will dissolve your heart with love.* This is the kind of dialogue that calls for economy, courtesy, and reverence in the language we use. If we speak too long, too overbearingly, or too factually, we will never help the lovers get together. Our job is to choose the fewest, best words that will allow them to find one another and then to get out of the way.

That is really all I mean by economy: to say only what we know to be true, to say it from the heart, and to sit down. In a time of famine, it is more important than ever to set a simple table. A preacher does not have to be a gourmet cook, whipping up cream sauces and stuffing squash blossoms with wild mushroom mousse. Hungry people may sicken on a meal like that. What they need are fresh ingredients in small portions. The clearer the broth, the better.

In a word-clogged world, the only words that stand a chance of getting people's attention are simple, honest words that come from everyday life. Most of us are "damaged trusters" where language is concerned. We have been seduced and dumped by language, we have been bullied and tricked.

When people come at us with words, we would like them to hold their hands out first where we can see them, to check for weapons. We would like them to keep their distance until we have had a chance to sniff the air for explosives.

Our listeners are no different, and they do not grow new ears when they walk into church. They are on the defensive, most of them. They reserve the right to decide for themselves whether or not what we say is true, and they will base that decision only partly on the content of our speech. Far more important than that is their reading of our congruity. Does what we say match up with how we are saying it? Do we look as if we live in the same world they do? Are we going to tell the truth about that world or are we going to pretend?

From the moment we open our mouths to speak, people collect data about our reliability from our faces, our bodies, our voices, our clothes. These are all parts of the language we speak, and we will not gain a full hearing until our listeners have learned enough from them to decide whether or not we are trustworthy. This may be as good a reason to preach a long sermon as a short one, but in a time of famine I am more interested than ever in the art of the homily. Again, this is a famine typified not by too little but by too much. There are mountains of junk food around, sealed in foil packages with expired dates stamped on them. What are scarce are sources of real nourishment—fresh brown rolls with no wrappers at all.

Anyone who speaks knows that it is more difficult to compose a short speech than a long one. To focus on one theme, to allow no digressions, to choose only the best words, to strive for clarity of thought and simplicity of expression, bringing the whole thing home in ten minutes or less—that is much harder work than taking twice that long to layer frosting on the cake. The only reason to attempt it, as far as I can tell, is that the quality of attention brought to a short sermon tends to exceed that brought to a long one. The less one is offered, the more one may savor. There is also less opportunity to doze. Congregations conditioned to long sermons with summaries at the end soon learn there is no danger they will miss anything. They need only "come to" for the final paragraph.

Another reason to craft shorter sermons is to leave more room for other elements of worship. The way many of our services are designed, the spotlight is on the preacher, with sometimes disastrous results for congregational life and the preacher's own sense of importance. On what grounds is a sermon more essential to the salvation of souls than the public reading of scripture, corporate prayers, or the recital of the church's faith in psalms and hymns? In a world drowning in noise, what could be more redemptive than a few moments of hallowed silence? Different churches have different customs, and I have heard forty-minute sermons I wished would never end. On the whole, however, I believe many of us do more honor to the Word of God by saying less instead of more.

In an essay on his fellow poet Robert Frost, W. H. Auden once noted a quality of what he called "auditory chastity" in Frost's poetry. The language, he said, is simple. "There is not a word, not a historical or literary reference in the whole of his work which would be strange to an unbookish boy of fifteen."[7] And yet Frost manages to express a great range of experience and emotion with his simple speech. The passion is there, but "the saying is reticent," so that the words bloom more in the ear than in the mouth.

At this point, I am more interested in Auden's phrase than in Frost's poetry. *Auditory chastity.* What a charming notion for those who wish to honor God's silence in their speech. It is also counter-cultural, insofar as language in our culture is anything but chaste. What would it mean for us to practice chastity in our preaching—to make modest proposals in the simplest language available, to trust the influence of unsullied speech?

In August of 1995, my telephone rang late one Saturday night. The caller was a teenaged boy who said he wanted to add someone to the parish prayer list. "Tomorrow," he said, "when we pray for those who have died, will you please pray for Jerry Garcia?" For one ridiculous moment I tried to place Jerry in my congregation. Was he a newcomer? Then my fog cleared and I realized we were talking about the lead guitarist for the Grateful Dead, who had just died in a California drug treatment center. Because the boy was genuinely grief-stricken, I said I would pray for Jerry on Sunday and I did.

It was not until four months later that I thought of him again, when I read Ken Kesey's eulogy for Garcia in the year-end issue of *The New York Times Magazine*. "Hey, Jerry—" the piece began, and then went on to praise Garcia's own auditory chastity.

"You could be a sharp-tongued popper of balloons when you were so inclined," Kesey wrote. "You were the sworn enemy of hot air and commercials, however righteous the cause or lucrative the product. Nobody ever heard you use that microphone as a pulpit.... No trendy spins. No bayings of belief. And if you did have any dogma, you surely kept it tied up under the back porch, where a smelly old hound belongs.... It was the false notes you didn't play that kept that lead line so golden pure. It was the words you didn't sing."[8]

Whatever you think of Kesey's aesthetic, he is telling us something important about the large numbers of people who loved Garcia and his music. *Nobody ever heard you use that microphone as a pulpit.* What is the difference between the two? Hot air and commercials, says Kesey. False notes too easily played. We do not have to take this personally, but if we do then there is something here for those of us who preach, if only in the metaphor. If we want to keep the golden lead line pure, there are some words we will not sing.

Or, as a friend of mine puts it, "I wish someone would tell preachers not to lie. It is better to tell your own pitiful story, whatever that may be, than to puff it up by lying." For her, lying not only means pretending to know the mind of God when you barely know your own or trying to persuade people that Christianity is a safe and easy way to live. It also means passing other people's language off as your own. As far as my friend is concerned, borrowed language is not worth the breath required to produce it. The least a preacher can do is to reach for his or her own words, fresh from the world in which ordinary people live. Secondary sources are welcome as long as they have passed through the preacher's own mind and heart. The point is to speak in an authentic voice, so that those who have all but lost their trust in the spoken word find reason to listen, even a little, to someone who sounds as if he or she has genuinely covered the territory.

Some of you know of the poet and naturalist Gary Snyder, who won a Pulitzer prize in 1975. I especially love an essay of his called "Crawling," in which he describes moving on his belly through a forest in the Sierra. Since the forest there is checkered with patches that have been burned or logged and are now almost impassable with thick new growth, most hikers stick to the old logging roads or trails. Pioneer that he is, Snyder preferred the road less traveled and set off through the woods on his hands and knees. Shimmying under fallen trunks and squirming his way through fields of prickly manzanita, he was always happy to find a patch of snow that would let him slide on his belly for a ways. At one point he came face to face with a pile of steaming bear scat and, a little further on, with a prize boletus mushroom. "You can *smell* the fall mushrooms when crawling," he wrote. "You brush cool dew off a young fir with your face."[9] The trick, he says, is to have no attachment to standing, to trade that in on a desire to explore the world up close.

Reading him, I decided he was a good homiletics instructor. What would our sermons sound like if we approached the text that way? What kind of revelations are we missing in this world because we insist on walking upright, while so much life takes place closer to the ground? In a time of famine, our role as scouts has grown more serious than ever. Hungry people have no use for agricultural analysts. They need someone actively involved in the search for food. It is not enough for us to claim to know people who knew people who once crawled on their bellies before God. Our job is to be those people ourselves, exploring the territory on our own hands and knees so that we do not miss a single mushroom. When we stand up to speak, it would be good for us to have twigs in our hair—better yet, an alarming shine on our faces—so that our listeners know where we have been (and whom we have sought) on their behalf.

If we really love them, we won't bring them back much to eat. If we did that, they might mistake us for the Food Giver. Each of us has the opportunity to reverse what happened at Mount Sinai, if we dare. Instead of volunteering to protect the people from God, we can step aside. We can invite them to go explore the territory for themselves, offering to crawl alongside them if they wish, until they discover whatever it is God gives them to discover. Our speech does not have to be polished at this point. It simply has to be true—not true about God, necessarily (how would we know?), but true about what it is to be human and hungry in a fallen world full of wonders.

Since such speech is the very definition of courtesy, let me move from the broad topic of economy in language to the equally broad topic of courtesy in our language about holy things. By courtesy, I mean the opposite of coercion. Courteous language respects the autonomy of the hearer. It also respects his or her ability to make meaning without too much supervision, which means it is language with some silence in it. A courteous preacher knows the importance of leaving partly described what can only be partly described. Even Ezekiel, when he had done his best to portray the four living creatures who flapped their sixteen wings in his bedazzled face, had the courtesy to say, "This was the appearance of the likeness of the glory of the LORD" (1:28).

He knew better than to say more than that. More than that would have been presumptuous, even though he had just gone into exquisite detail about the vision he had seen. Over the heads of the living creatures was "something like a dome, shining like crystal." When the creatures stretched out their wings, the sound under that dome was like the sound of mighty waters, like the thunder of the Almighty. Above the dome was "something like a throne, in appearance like sapphire; and seated above the likeness of a throne was something that seemed like a human form." Fire and splendor enclosed it all around. It was "like the bow in a cloud on a rainy day, such was the appearance of the splendor all around. This was the appearance of the likeness of the glory of the LORD" (Ezekiel 1:4-28).

There was no hiding of the divine face from Ezekiel. He both saw it and heard it, but the privilege of that full revelation did not include the words to describe it. His account is packed with similes—twenty-two of them in twenty-four verses—*something like four living creatures, something like a wheel within a wheel, something like a throne.* These approximations are as far as Ezekiel will go. He will not even say, *exactly like.* The vision exceeds his ability to say it, but it is more than that. With the language he has, he will not trespass upon the silence of God. There are things no mortal should say, even if one sees them and is allowed to live through them. Where the glory of the Lord is concerned, *something like* is as close as humans may come.

In a time of famine typified by too many words with too much noise in them, we could use fewer words with more silence in them. This is a difficult concept to grasp, but you know it when you hear it. Some of the most effective language in the world leads you up to the brink of silence and leaves you there, with the soft surf of the unsayable lapping at your feet. I am thinking of the silence to which Dante surrendered his love of Beatrice. In the twenty-third canto of *Paradiso*, he did the best he could. "It seemed to me her face was all aflame," he wrote, "and there was so much gladness in her eyes—I am compelled to leave it undescribed."[10]

The word gives way to silence, engaging the hearer in a way more words could not have done. Jesus practiced this art as well as anyone ever has. He spoke, and there was silence. Whether he was giving moral instruction or describing the kingdom with the "something likes" of his ancestor Ezekiel, he produced silence in his listeners—usually by confounding their expectations in a way that emptied their heads right out. He knew how to stop talking while people were still listening. He got them following behind him until they were going about sixty miles an hour and then he turned off the road, watching their surprised faces as they whizzed right by without him.

His use of story and image were central to his strategy. Both left room for his listeners to take part in the making of their meaning, especially the ones he left unfinished. A story such as the prodigal son does not have one ending but two or three, depending on the listener. Even one as finished as the story of the sower leaves room for the listener to decide: What kind of soil am I? There is no hogging of the hermeneutic here. The speaker and the listener are full partners in the unfolding of the truth.

Since there is no shortage of available comment on Jesus' narrative style, I will not make more of it here, except to point out how *courteous* it is, how respectful of the listener. Story and image both have great pockets of silence in them. They do not come at the ear the same way advice and exhortation do—although they are, I believe, even more persuasive. Perhaps that is because they create a quiet space where one may lay down one's defenses for a while. A story does not ask for decision. Instead, it asks for identification, which is how transformation begins.

The best stories and images are those that have the most recognizable life in them, which means that they are rarely simple or neat. I worry sometimes that much of what people hear in church is the cartoon version of real life—sermons populated with one-dimensional characters who work out their problems without ever using language that might threaten their rating. Meanwhile, many of our listeners are the same people who pay good money to go see movies such as *Slingblade* or *The Company of Men*, which—for all their rawness—have provoked more moral discourse among more people than any sermon I can think of at the moment. At least part of the reason, I believe, is that they do not come with morals attached. It is up to the viewer to make the meaning.

Fortunately, the Bible is full of such raw and powerful stories. Maybe we should preach more of them, and where they are obscure, troubling, or incomplete, perhaps we should leave them that way. Who are we, after all, to defend God? Once, after the composer Robert Schumann had played a particularly difficult étude, he was asked by a member of his audience please to explain it. In reply, Schumann sat down and played it again. We could do worse than to follow his example when we come to particularly difficult pieces of God's music. Our job is not always to explain them. Sometimes it is enough to play them again so that they are heard in all their tooth-rattling dissonance. The discord—like the silence—is God's problem, not ours. When we try to solve it, we are no longer being courteous. We are once again reaching for the fruit of the tree of the knowledge of good and evil, the taste of which we cannot seem to get out of our mouths.

Which brings me to my last point on homiletical restraint, reverence, which is the best reason of all to limit our speech. When we go on and on about things, we develop what Susan Sontag calls an "ontological stammer."[11] Our anxiety shows, as well as our ignorance. It is enough for us to discern the limits of what is sayable and then to pour our energy into saying it as economically, as courteously, and as reverently as we can. When we stop talking, it is not because there is no more to be said. It is because the unsayable wishes to be said, and the only language for saying that is silence. Once, when he was too ill to preach, Saint Francis simply stood before his congregation—mute—and gazed on them with love.

Too often, I believe, preachers get into the business of giving answers instead of ushering people into the presence of the God who may or may not answer. We have somehow fallen into the trap of believing that we are responsible for God's silence—that if those under our care do not have a sense of God's presence, then it is because we have failed them somehow—failed at Bible study, failed at prayer, failed in our preaching to bring the invisible God close enough to touch. When God falls silent, we too often compensate by talking more, which may the very worst thing we can do.

Who are we, to insert ourselves between God's silence and those for whom the silence is intended?

We *are* responsible for doing our best to put all the tools of communication with God where our congregations can reach them and for demonstrating their use in our own lives. After that, the matter is out of our hands. Only an idol always answers. The true God possesses more freedom than that, and I believe we do more for those in our care by teaching them about the silence of God than we do by trying to explain it away. By addressing the experience of God's silence in scripture and in our listeners' own lives, we may be able to open up the possibility that silence is as much a sign of God's presence as of God's absence—that divine silence is not a vacuum to be filled but a mystery to be entered into, unarmed with words and undistracted by noise—a holy of holies in which we too may be struck dumb by the power of the unsayable God.

Our job is not to pierce that mystery with language but to reverence it. Our understanding, such as it is, is never a result of trespassing the bounds of the holy but of knowing where they are, and of having the good sense not to say what cannot be said. Within this understanding, the failure of our speech is not something to be dreaded but something to be hoped for. It means that we have encountered the transcendent God, whose sound cannot be imitated. In order for us to hear it, all mediators must hush.

Jesus came among us as word. I believe God remains among us as music (and the Holy Spirit as the breath that brings both word and music to life). Those of us who preach may never stop judging ourselves for failing to do justice to the Word, but how can we ever do justice to the Music? How would you preach a sermon on Barber's Adagio or the slow movement of Schubert's C-Major quintet? Would you hum? Snap your fingers? How does the human voice capture the sound of sobbing violins? And yet that is what we are up against as we try to toss the fragile nets of our words over the bone-melting, universe-making music of God.

We are not excused from trying, only from succeeding. Meanwhile we do the best we can, taking up the soiled, tired language we have been given and asking God to give us grace as well, that we might by our tender, devoted handling of those words be able to bring a few of them back to life.

But only a few. In a way that surpasses understanding, our duty in this time of famine is not to end the human hunger and thirst for God's word but to intensify it, until the whole world bangs its forks for God's food. That is what the famine is for, according to scripture. That is why God has hidden God's face: to increase our sense of loss until we are so hungry and lonely for God that we do something about it—not only one by one but also as a people who are once again ready to leave our fleshpots in search of real food.

Whatever preachers serve on Sunday, it must not blunt the appetite for this food. If people go away from us full, then we have done them a disservice. What we serve is not supposed to satisfy. It is food for the journey. It is meant to tantalize, to send people out our doors with a taste for what they cannot find in our kitchens. When they find it, they understand why we did not say more about it than we did. It was not that we didn't. It was that we couldn't.

Our words are too fragile. God's silence is too deep. But oh, what gorgeous sounds our failures make: words flung against the silence like wine glasses pitched against a hearth. As lovely as they are, they were meant for smashing. For when they do, it is as if a little of God's own music breaks through.

Endnotes

1. Donald W. McCullough, *The Trivialization of God: The Dangerous Illusion of a Manageable Deity* (Colorado Springs: NavPress, 1995), 77.

2. Blaise Pascal, *Thoughts*, trans. W. F. Trotter (New York: Collier, 1910), 195.

3. *The Essential Rumi*, trans. Coleman Barks with John Moyne, A. J. Arberry, and Reynold Nicholson (HarperSanFrancisco, 1995), 24.

4. Martin Buber, *The Eclipse of God: Studies in the Relation Between Religion and Philosophy* (Atlantic Highlands, N.J.: Humanities Press International, Inc., 1988), 7-8.

5. James Breech, *The Silence of Jesus: The Authentic Voice of the Historical Man* (Philadelphia: Fortress Press, 1983), 4.

6. Max Picard, *The World of Silence* (Chicago: Henry Regnery Company, 1952), 5, 165.

7. W. H. Auden, *The Dyer's Hand and Other Essays* (New York: Vintage Books, 1968), 342-343.

8. Ken Kesey, "The False Notes He Never Played," *The New York Times Magazine* (December 31, 1995), 20.

9. Gary Snyder, *A Place in Space: Ethics, Aesthetics and Watersheds* (Washington, D. C.: Counterpoint, 1995), 194.

10. Dante, *Paradiso: Third Book of The Divine Comedy*, trans. Allen Mandelbaum (Berkeley: University of California Press, 1982), 200.

11. Susan Sontag, "The Aesthetics of Silence," *The Susan Sontag Reader* (New York: Farrar/Straus/Giroux, 1982), 199.

Sources Consulted

Auden, W. H. *The Dyer's Hand and Other Essays.*
New York: Vintage Books, 1968.

Breech, James. *The Silence of Jesus: The Authentic
Voice of the Historical Man.* Philadelphia:
Fortress Press, 1983.

Brook, Peter. *The Empty Space.* New York:
Atheneum, 1968.

Buber, Martin. *The Eclipse of God: Studies in the
Relation between Religion & Philosophy.* Atlantic

Highlands, New Jersey: Humanities Press International, 1988.

Cage, John. *Silence: Lectures and Writings by John Cage.* Middletown, Connecticut: Wesleyan University Press, 1973.

Carse, James. *The Silence of God: Meditations on Prayer.* San Francisco: HarperSanFranciso, 1995.

Coggan, Donald. *Preaching: The Sacrament of the Word.* New York: Crossroad Publishing Company, 1988.

Courtenay, Charles. *The Empire of Silence.* New York: Sturgis & Walton Company, 1916.

Craddock, Fred B. *Preaching.* Nashville: Abingdon Press, 1985.

Crossan, John Dominic. *The Dark Interval: Toward a Theology of Story*. Sonoma, California: Polebridge Press, 1988.

Dante. *Paradiso: Third Book of The Divine Comedy*, translated by Allen Mandelbaum. Berkeley, California: University of California Press, 1982.

Decker, Bert. *You've Got To Be Believed To Be Heard*. New York: Saint Martin's Press, 1991.

DeWailly, L. M. "The Silence of the Word," in *The Word: Readings in Theology*, 286-297. New York: P. J. Kennedy & Sons, 1964.

Friedman, Richard Elliott. *The Disappearance of God: A Divine Mystery*. New York: Little Brown and Company, 1995. (This book has been reissued in paperback as *The Hidden Face of God*.)

Iyer, Pico. "The Eloquent Sounds of Silence," *Time* (January 25, 1993), 74.

Lash, Nicholas. *The Beginning and the End of 'Religion'*. Cambridge, England: Cambridge University Press, 1996.

Laurence, Patricia Ondek. *The Reading of Silence: Virginia Woolf in the English Tradition*. Stanford: Stanford University Press, 1991.

Lewis, C. S. *Studies in Words*. New York: Cambridge University Press, 1960.

McCullough, Donald W. *The Trivialization of God: The Dangerous Illusion of a Manageable Deity*. Colorado Springs: NavPress, 1995.

Merton, Thomas. *The Springs of Contemplation*. Notre Dame: Ave Maria Press, 1992.

Mitchell, Stephen. *The Book of Job*. San Francisco: North Point Press, 1979.

Neher, Andre. *The Exile of the Word: From the Silence of the Bible to the Silence of Auschwitz.* Philadelphia: The Jewish Publication Society of America, 5741/1981.

Percy, Walker. *The Message in the Bottle.* New York: Farrar, Straus and Giroux, 1975.

Picard, Max. *The World of Silence.* Chicago: Henry Regnery Company, 1952.

Rilke, Rainer Maria. *The Duino Elegies.* New York: W. W. Norton & Company, Inc., 1963.

Rumi, Jelaluddin. *The Essential Rumi,* trans. Coleman Barks with John Moyne, A. J. Arberry and Reynold Nicholson. San Francisco: HarperSanFrancisco, 1995.

Safire, William. *The First Dissident: The Book of Job in Today's Politics.* New York: Random House, 1992.

Sells, Michael A. *Mystical Languages of Unsaying.* Chicago: The University of Chicago Press, 1994.

Snyder, Gary. *A Place in Space: Ethics, Aesthetics and Watersheds.* Washington, D. C.: Counterpoint, 1995.

Sontag, Susan. "The Aesthetics of Silence," in *The Susan Sontag Reader*, 181-204. New York: Farrar/Straus/Giroux, 1982.

Steiner, George. *Language & Silence: Essays on Language, Literature and the Inhuman.* New York: Atheneum, 1986.

Steiner, George. *Real Presences.* Chicago: The University of Chicago Press, 1989.

Stevens, Wallace. *The Necessary Angel: Essays on Reality and the Imagination.* New York: Vintage Books, 1951.

Sources Consulted

Wolpe, David J. *In Speech and In Silence: The Jewish Quest for God*. New York: Henry Holt and Company, 1992.

Cowley Publications is a ministry of the Society of St. John the Evangelist, a religious community for men in the Episcopal Church. Emerging from the Society's tradition of prayer, theological reflection, and diversity of mission, the press is centered in the rich heritage of the Anglican Communion.

Cowley Publications seeks to provide books, audio cassettes, and other resources for the ongoing theological exploration and spiritual development of the Episcopal Church and others in the body of Christ. To this end, it is dedicated to developing a new generation of theological writers, encouraging them to produce timely, creative, and stimulating publications of excellence, and making these publications available widely, reaching both clergy and lay persons.